for Prism
Premiered November 19, 2004 at Symphony Space, New York Ci

Scherzino

Alto Saxophone in E♭

WILLIAM BOLCOM
2004

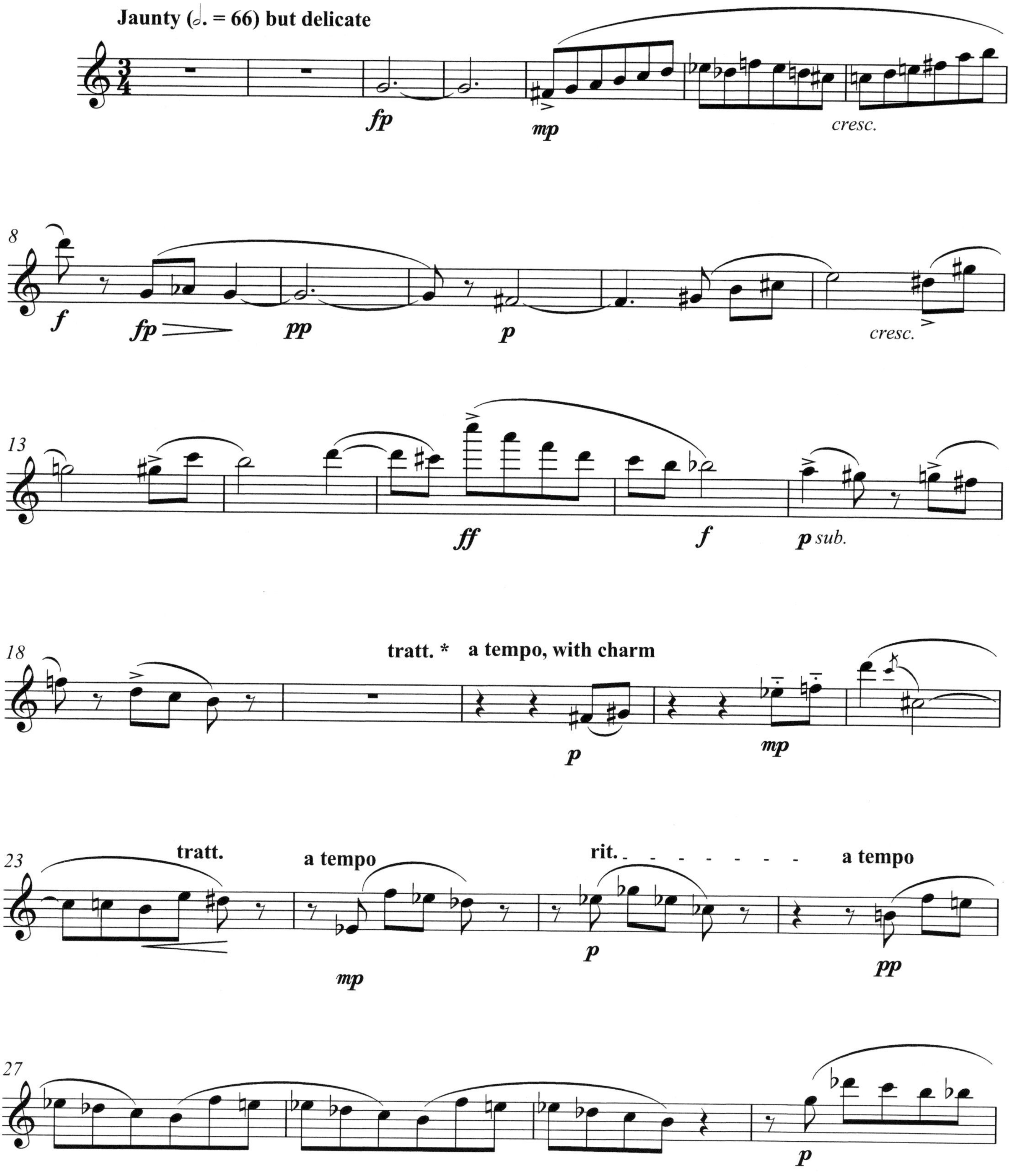

*trattenuto = just slightly held back

Alto Saxophone in E♭

Scherzino

WILLIAM BOLCOM

31
mf
p
36
pp
tratt.
a tempo
p
p
40
mp
fp
44
pp
tratt.
a tempo
fp
pp
fp
p
fp
49
p
ff
p
pp
54
mp
mf
G.P.
(in time)
59
p
pp
sempre pp
64
molto
gl.
ff